Venus
The Masked Planet

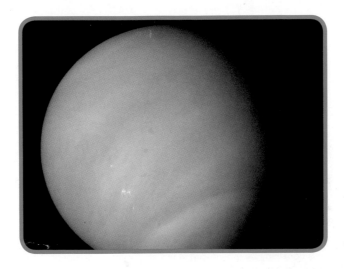

By Lincoln James

Gareth Stevens
Publishing

Please visit our Web site, www.garethstevens.com. For a free color catalog of all our high-quality books, call toll free 1-800-542-2595 or fax 1-877-542-2596.

Library of Congress Cataloging-in-Publication Data

James, Lincoln.
    Venus : the masked planet / Lincoln James.
        p. cm. — (Our solar system)
    Includes bibliographical references and index.
    ISBN 978-1-4339-3846-7 (pbk.)
    ISBN 978-1-4339-3847-4 (6-pack)
    ISBN 978-1-4339-3845-0 (lib. bdg.)
    1. Venus (Planet)—Juvenile literature. I. Title.
    QB621.J26 2011
    523.42—dc22

                                        2010000486

First Edition

Published in 2011 by
Gareth Stevens Publishing
111 East 14th Street, Suite 349
New York, NY 10003

Designer: Daniel Hosek
Editor: Greg Roza

Photo credits: Cover, back cover, pp. 1, 15, 17 (Venus) NASA; pp. 5, 9 Shutterstock.com; p. 7 Mike Hewitt/Getty Images; p. 11 David Cortner/NASA; pp. 13 (top), 19, 21 NASA/JPL; p. 13 (bottom) © Photodisc; p. 17 (sun) © Digital Vision.

Printed in the United States of America

CPSIA compliance information: Batch #CS10GS: For further information contact Gareth Stevens, New York, New York at 1-800-542-2595.

Contents

Boldface words appear in the glossary.

Close Neighbor

The second planet from the sun in our **solar system** is Venus. It comes closer to Earth than any other planet. Venus is a little smaller than Earth.

Our Solar System

Neptune

Uranus

Saturn

Mars

Venus

Jupiter

Earth

Mercury

sun

5

We can see Venus from Earth without a **telescope**! Venus is one of the brightest objects in the night sky. Only the moon is brighter.

moon

Venus

7

Venus can often be seen just before sunrise and just after sunset. Sometimes it is called the Morning Star. Sometimes it is called the Evening Star.

Moving Through Space

All of the planets in the solar system **orbit** the sun. Venus orbits the sun once every 225 days.

sun

Venus

Venus spins in the **opposite** direction from the other planets. It also spins much more slowly than the other planets. It makes one full turn every 243 days.

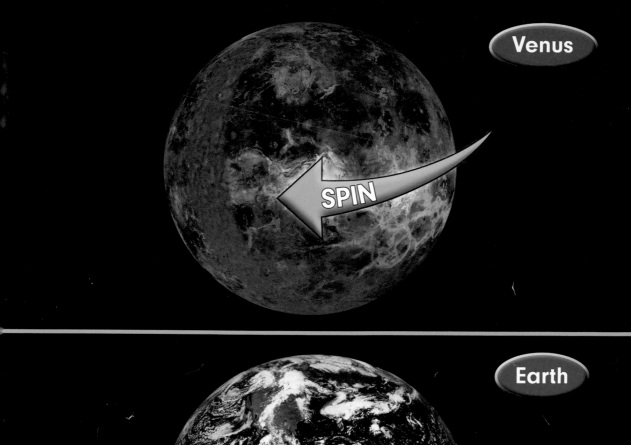

Venus

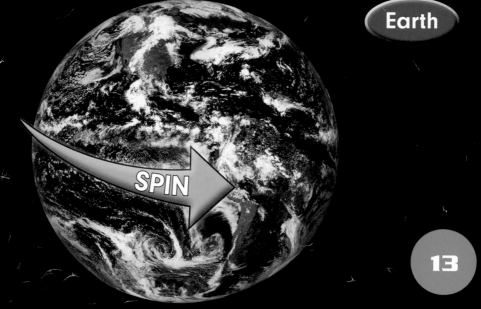

Earth

13

The Clouds of Venus

Venus is covered by thick clouds. The clouds are like a mask that hides the planet. They are not like the clouds on Earth. They are filled with harmful gases!

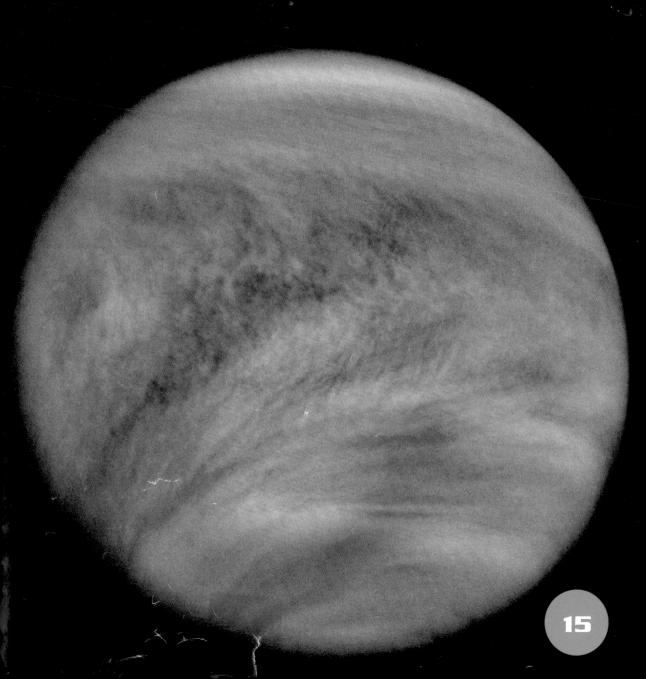

Venus's thick clouds trap the sun's heat. This makes Venus the hottest planet in the solar system. It can get twice as hot as the oven in your kitchen!

Beneath the Clouds

Venus has mountains and plains. Its land is very hot and dry. Scientists think it was shaped a long time ago by **volcanoes**.

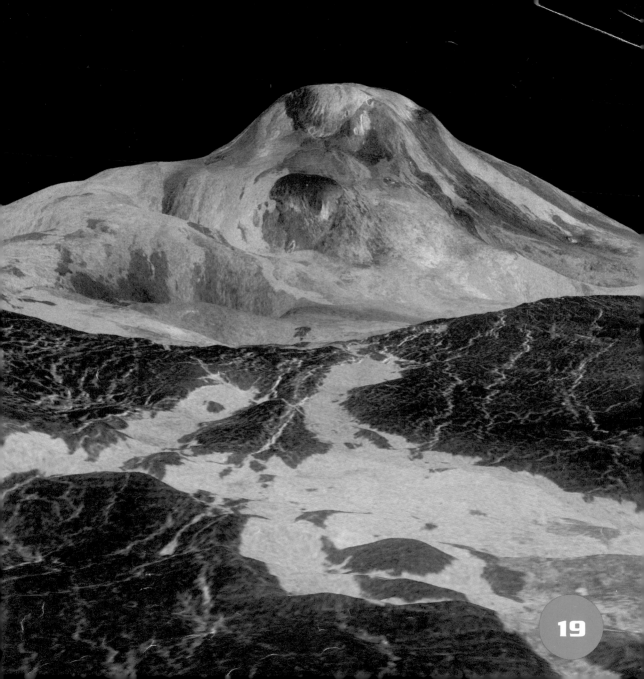

Looking Under the Mask

Scientists use telescopes and other special tools to see through the clouds that mask Venus. They hope to learn even more about Venus and how it formed.

Glossary

opposite: going the other way

orbit: to travel in a circle or oval around something else

solar system: the sun and all the space objects that orbit it, including the planets and their moons

telescope: a tool that makes faraway objects look larger and closer

volcano: an opening in a planet's surface through which hot, liquid rock sometimes flows

For More Information

Books

Chrismer, Melanie. *Venus*. Danbury, CT: Children's Press, 2008.

Wimmer, Teresa. *Venus*. Mankato, MN: Creative Education, 2007.

Web Sites

Venus

www.kidsastronomy.com/venus.htm
Read interesting facts about Venus and find links to the other planets.

Venus: The Hottest Planet

solarsystem.nasa.gov/planets/profile.cfm?Object=Venus&Display=Kids
NASA's Web page on Venus covers basic facts about the planet and the missions to study it.

Index

About the Author

Lincoln James is a retired aerospace engineer and amateur astronomer living in St. Augustine, Florida. He enjoys building miniature rockets with his four sons and taking family trips to the Kennedy Space Center to watch space shuttle launches.